A Basic Approach to Quality Control and SPC

A Basic Approach
to Quality Control
and SPC

Peter D. Mauch

Authors Choice Press
New York   Bloomington

Authors Choice Press
An imprint of iUniverse, Inc.

For information address:
iUniverse
1663 Liberty Drive
Bloomington, IN 47403
www.iuniverse.com
1-800-Authors (1-800-288-4677)

ISBN: 978-1-4401-2796-0

Printed in the United States of America

Contents

Preface..**vii**

Chapter 1

Introduction to the Quality Sciences... 1

  What is Quality?.. 1

    Unified Quality Theory.. 2

      How Does Quality Apply? 4

      Business Modeling... 5

      Inputs 5

      Transformation 6

      Quality Organization's Role..10

Chapter 2

Defining the Product 13

  Attributes...15

  Variables 16

  Operating Conditions 17

  Review 18

Chapter 3

Defining the Process..19

  Organizational Chart 19

  Material Flow Diagrams..22

  Simplified Block Diagrams 24

  Review 26

Chapter 4

Problem Solving 27

  Problem-Solving Techniques...27

  Problem Scenario..28

  Identification of the Problem 28

  Gathering Data..30

Analysis of the Data 31
Developing Solutions 31
Developing a Plan 31
Implementing the Plan 33
Corrections to the Plan 33
Review 33

Chapter 5
Statistical Methods 35
    Measures of Location 36
    Measures of Variation 38
    Control Charts 39
    Control Limits for Sample Averages 42
    Control Limits for Sample Ranges 42
    Instructions for Control Chart Preparation 43
        Variable Control Charts 43
        Attribute Control Charts 50
    Analysis of Control Charts 59

Appendix 61

Index 63

Preface

This book comprises five sections. Each section aims to help the reader understand the steps needed to develop a detection-oriented quality system for operations. The five sections are briefly described below:

- **Chapter 1: Quality**

  In this chapter, the reader is introduced to the fundamental concept of quality and its relationship to other departments in the business organization.

- **Chapter 2: Defining the Product**

  The manner in which quality groups define products with the use of marketing, engineering, and customer information is explained in this chapter.

- **Chapter 3: Defining the Process**

  Some of the techniques used to describe various processes, from material flow to block diagrams of machines, are explored in this chapter.

- **Chapter 4: Problem Solving**

  Basic principles for scientific problem solving are covered in this chapter.

- **Chapter 5: Statistical Methods**

  Concepts for control charting, including variable and attribute techniques along with the necessary theory, are presented in this chapter.

This book will provide the reader with the tools needed to develop a statistical process control program with the use of control charts. It is important to remember that the use of statistics is not confined to these few applications. Many techniques are used for detailed analysis. As you master each one, you will gain confidence in your decision-making ability, thereby reducing the risk of error.

This book will guide you into the larger world of quality science. From here, you can progress to and discover the rewards that result from providing the best possible product and the lowest cost ... in short, making our society a better place to live.

Chapter 1

INTRODUCTION TO THE QUALITY SCIENCES

The definition of quality varies from person to person. Some see quality as the value of an item, and others see quality as perfection; still others see quality as a defect-free product.

What Is Quality?

When it comes to business and its operation, quality must be viewed in terms of performance. Types of performance measurement vary greatly among business professionals. The current standard for measurement of business performance is through financial means. In short, the difference between profit and loss reflects the success rate. A difference of opinion exists, however, as to whether financial measures truly indicate a company's performance.

Financial performance indicators only reflect the outcome of business operations. A business can remain solvent for a period of time before declines in revenue begin to affect its survival. If a business generates only $50,000 in sales for the first two months of a new year and its yearly operating expenses are $25,000, it would show a net gain of $25,000, even if no sales occurred during the remainder of the year. Obviously, financial measures of performance are inadequate in this case. Financial performance indicators do not reflect the efficacy of business operations management.

The main purpose of a business is to provide a product(s) or service(s) to satisfy some external need. A business cannot service itself; it must service an external customer or need, in exchange for resources needed for operation. Quality, in this sense, is the business' performance in satisfying those external needs. Quality, therefore, is "the efficiency of a business system to meet external needs."

1

The role of the quality department is to identify, analyze, summarize, and report the efficiency of the business system to meet external needs. In addition, the quality group may be called on to provide performance planning, performance improvement, and performance control of the business system. Ultimately, the senior management staff is responsible for the performance of their business system in much the same way that they are responsible for the management of company financial resources.

The key to business system performance is in the level at which the various departments responsible for product development integrate. Product development departments (mainly marketing, engineering, and production) must interact effectively to meet external needs. In addition, these groups must have optimum internal tasking with checks and balances. In other words, each product development department must continually seek ways to improve its internal performance and interface with other product development departments.

The organization of a company can dramatically affect business system performance. If departments are organized in such a way that their objectives conflict, an informal suborganization will emerge whose hidden objectives will oppose or compete with company goals. When this occurs, business efficiency to meet external needs declines, leading to decreased revenue. As the efficiency to meet external needs declines, an associated decrease in sales occurs within six months to two years.

The lag between the decline in efficiency and decreased sales is due to efforts by management to reduce direct costs (labor and material) and ineffective market promotional efforts. These efforts result in accelerated decline, due largely to the fact that performance planning and control are not affected.

Regardless of the product or service a business provides, three basic groups emerge: decision makers, product developers, and internal analyzers. Each group has specific, significantly different objectives. Any mixing of these groups, such as the placement of the Accounting Department under Production, causes decreased business efficiency. Similarly, placement of the Marketing Department under Human Resources would cause the same conflict in objectives, leading to decreased business efficiency. Accordingly, placement of the Quality Department under Production will have the same effect. Figure 1 and Table 1 show the relationship between decision makers, product developers, and internal analyzers.

Unified Quality Theory

During the past 20 years, chief executive officers have discovered that financial indicators are poor measures of corporate performance. Financial reports can only identify a problem, as poor earnings are a sign of serious root problems in a company. Questions remain: "How is corporate performance

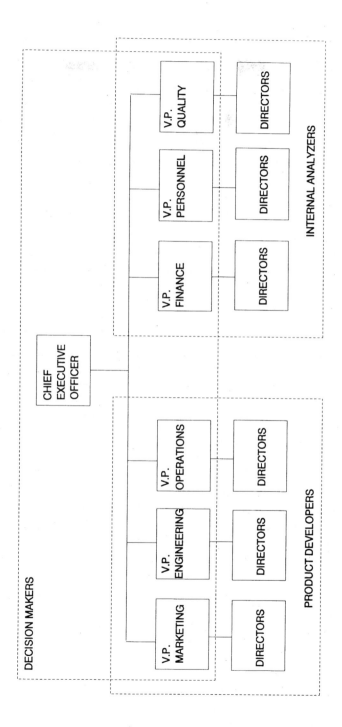

Figure 1: Business Department Relationships

Table 1: Business Elements

Organizational System Elements:	Organizational systems comprise internal interdependent components or subparts. The organization also has the capacity for feedback, equilibrium, and equifinality.
Decision Makers:	Managers responsible for resource allocation and configuration to implement a strategy and produce effective organizational, group/unit, and individual performance.
Product Developers:	Those groups/units within the organization that develop, transform, or provide output.
Internal Analyzers:	Those groups/units within the organization that provide feedback on the performance of the organizational system.

accurately measured?" Even more important, "How is a company turned around once economic symptoms become present?" There has been a proliferation of quick-fix ideas to turn a company around, the most notable of which result in "management bashing" or, more simply put, replacement of mid-level managers who appear to be poor performers.

Chief executive officers have a problem using the skills of the quality professional due to a conflicting view of their role as problem solvers. For the most part, they view the quality organization as a means of control. In fact, many business texts include the quality organization in the control function of business operations management. Obviously, this provides most managers with a distorted understanding of the quality organization's objectives. Coupled with product-oriented definitions of quality, which further delineate the quality organization's true function, this results in an ineffective group.

How Does Quality Apply?

Most business managers, when asked how quality applies to their business, will likely expound on the virtue of a product that satisfies the customer. This occurs because most literature written about quality focuses on the product or the process by which it is produced. In business, quality must be applied toward some business model. To describe quality before it is defined is akin to having an answer and finding the facts to fit it.

Because quality will be defined in relationship to business, the term "business" must be described. This might seem to be an easy term to define, but there are literally hundreds of business models from which to choose. Businesses are made up of groups of people striving to accomplish and acquire things that they could not accomplish or acquire individually. If you thought a company was in business just to make a profit, you are wrong! Most studies performed today indicate that people do not get into business for a profit. Rather, most people begin a business as a means of independence and self-expression.

Business Modeling

Any business model used to define quality must be quantitative for analysis work. Figure 1 lists organizational elements that are found in most businesses today. In short, a business comprises three core elements: decision makers, product developers, and internal analyzers. These elements are affected by inputs and the transformation structure. Dissection of a business would reveal that each group/subpart has a specific task orientation. For example, the marketing, engineering, and production groups are involved in generating a product or service. The accounting, quality and human resources groups monitor business performance. Finally, a group of individuals is responsible for the intergroup configuration and resource allocation to achieve effective organizational performance. The efficiency with which these three elements interact is affected by two factors: inputs and transformation.

Inputs

Inputs to the business (Table 2) and its components comprise four elements: environment, resources, history, and strategy. The environment includes factors over which the business has little or no control, such as the customers' needs and wants. Marketing groups can create desire but cannot create needs. Needs are inherent to the customer.

Resources used by the business and its components are limited, but their scope includes not only materials but also market recognition, good will, and human resources.

The past patterns (history) of organizational behavior affect the performance of the business system. Of course, environment, resources, and history have dramatic impacts on the strategies developed by the decision makers.

Table 2: Input Elements

Environment:	All factors, including institutions, groups, individuals, and events, outside the boundaries of the organization being analyzed but having a potential impact on that organization.
Resources:	Various assets that the organization has access to, including human resources, technology, capital, and information, as well as less-tangible resources (recognition in the market, etc.).
History:	The patterns of past behavior, activity, and effectiveness of the organization that may have an effect on current organizational functioning.
Strategy:	The stream of decisions made about how organizational resources will be configured against the demands, constraints, and opportunities within the context of history.

Transformation

The transformation process (Table 3 and Figure 2) relates to both intragroup and intergroup goal achievement methods and is associated with four elements: tasks, people, formal organization, and informal organization.

Traditional quality studies have explored the task function of the transformation process in great detail; however, more work is needed to provoke studies in the area of formal and informal organization. Behavioral scientists have studied formal and informal structures in business management systems for longer than 80 years.

Given this transformation model (Table 4 and Figure 3), the task of defining quality, in a business sense, becomes obvious. It is the efficiency of the business system to meet external needs to satisfy internal needs. Table 5 provides a detailed breakdown of this definition.

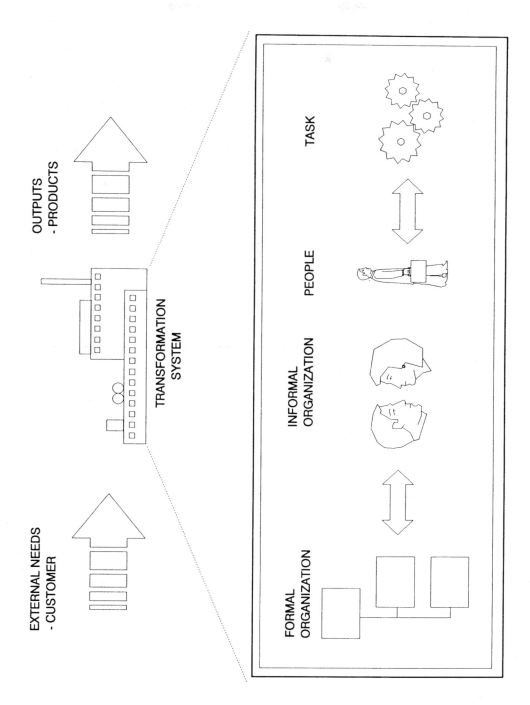

Figure 2: The transformation system in a business comprises a formal organization, informal organization, people, and tasks.

Table 3: Transformation Elements

Tasks:	The basic and inherent work to be done by the organization and its parts.
People:	The characteristics of individuals in the organization.
Formal Organization:	The various structures, processes, methods, etc., that are formally created to encourage individuals to perform tasks.
Informal Organization:	The emerging arrangements, including structures, processes, and relationships.

Table 4: Business Model

Organizational Model:	A business system model given a level abstraction for open systems, which reflects the basic system's concepts and characteristics but which is more usable as an analytical tool.
Inputs:	Those factors that are, at any time point, "givens" faced by the organization, including environment, resources, history, and strategy.
Transformation:	Those components within the organization that enable management — given an environment, a set of resources, and a history — to implement a strategy to produce effective organizational, group/unit, and individual performance. These components include the task, the people, the formal organization, and the informal organization.
Outputs:	What the organization produces, how it performs, or, globally, how effective it is, including goal attainment, resource utilization, and adaptability.

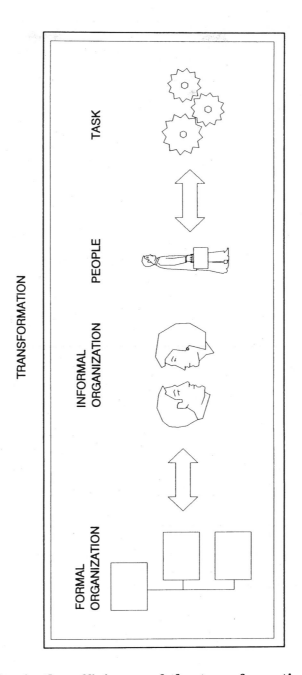

Figure 3: Quality is the efficiency of the transformation system to provide outputs that satisfy external needs. In the case of business: Quality is the efficiency of the transformation system to provide outputs that will satisfy customer needs.

Table 5: Unified Quality Theory

Quality:	The efficiency of a system to meet external needs.
Efficiency:	The degree to which the external needs and demands are met by the goals, objectives, and/or structures of the system.
System:	A set of interrelated elements that subjects environmental inputs to a transformation process and produces output.
External Needs:	The environmental requirements that must be satisfied to acquire benefits that cannot be achieved internally.

Quality Organization's Role

The role of the Quality Department is to identify, analyze, summarize, and report the performance of the business system and to require that the quality organization perform research and development of business performance. An example of this would be evaluation of prototypes to assess the performance of the engineering group. Quality audits also serve to monitor a system's performance level.

Because of the stereotypical picture associated with the term "quality control/assurance department," the term "performance research and development" better reflects the organization's role (Table 6 and Figure 4) and presents management with a clear understanding of the organization's objectives. A parallel to this would be the Accounting Department whose role is to monitor, report, and manage the financial performance of the business. Conversely, the performance research and development group monitors, reports, and manages business system efficiency.

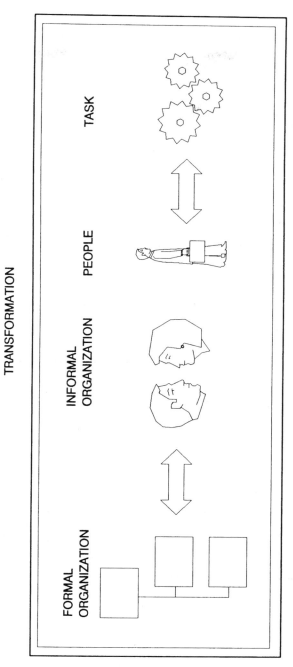

Figure 4: The role of the Quality Department is to identify, analyze, summarize, and report the efficiency (performance) of the system to meet external needs and to manage system improvement. In other words, business performance research and development.

Table 6:
Performance Research
and Development Department

Mission:	Identify, analyze, summarize, and report the efficiency of the business system, and manage and develop the means for performance improvement.
Performance Planning:	Identification of environmental elements outside the boundaries of the organization. Development of a strategy to utilize/configure the business system to satisfy the elements. Definition of a feedback system to verify the strategy performance.
Performance Improvement:	Identification of low-performance areas within the system. Formulation of a strategy to effect performance improvement. Implementation of the performance improvement action plans.
Performance Control:	Development of performance standards, measurement of variables, and measurement methods. Measurement of performance and reporting of departures from standards. System intervention to maintain standards.

Chapter 2

DEFINING THE PRODUCT

Because quality is the efficiency of a system to meet external needs, the needs must be described. This chapter will explore how to define external needs to evaluate how well your business systems have met them.

A few terms must be understood before the discussion begins:

Attribute:	A product feature or characteristic.
Variable:	A measureable product characteristic.
Operating Conditions:	The environment in which the product is expected to operate.
Critical Risk:	Any case where a deviation would cause a safety or health hazard or prevent the product from performing its basic function.
Major Risk:	Any case where a deviation would cause a substantial reduction in the product's ability to operate within the expected operating environment or is readily noticeable by the customer.
Minor Risk:	Any case where a deviation would not cause reduction in the product's operating conditions and is not readily noticeable by the customer.

The above terms are used to define the customers' requirements (external needs) (Figure 5). Business operations are evaluated based on these needs. This is the first essential step in planning control and improvements of business methods. A description of the product helps to eliminate waste and provides a more focused approach for those who do not have direct contact with the customer. It is also helpful to determine the appropriate actions to take when changes are needed.

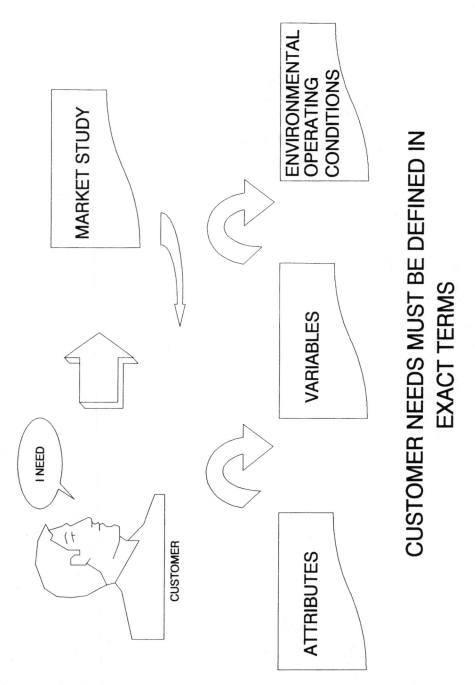

Figure 5: Quality specifications include attributes, variables, and environmental operating conditions.

To explain product definition, a plastic bag will be used as an example in this chapter. The plastic bag will be described and referred to later in this book. This will aid in a comparison of the bags manufactured with the product definition and an evaluation of the difference.

Many companies do not define their products. This causes confusion because everyone in the company has a different impression of what the product should be. When this occurs, employees spend time arguing about what the product should be, and, consequently, problems seldom get solved. To avoid this dilemma, products should be defined in exact terms.

Another aspect of product definition involves risk. Each characteristic or variable has an associated risk, relative to its importance in meeting customers' needs. Each product characteristic must be assigned a risk level based on how it will affect these needs.

A product is described with the following parameters: (1) attributes, (2) variables, and (3) operating conditions.

To explain how these parameters are used, each one will be explored in detail.

Attributes

Attributes are defined as product characteristics or features. For example, a carwash either waxes your car or it does not and a radio either plays in stereo or it does not. In the plastic bag example, the bag either leaks or it does not. Table 7 lists attributes of a plastic bag.

Table 7: Product Attributes of a Plastic Bag

Item	Characteristic	CR	MA	MI
1	Leakproof	XX		
2	See-through	XX		
3	Cleanliness		XX	

Table 7 lists the product attributes in their order of importance. On the right side of the table are the initials CR, MA, and MI, which indicate <u>cr</u>itical, <u>ma</u>jor, and <u>mi</u>nor, respectively. For each product feature, we have assigned a risk factor with regard to the needs.

In Table 7, no numbers have been assigned to the features. The product (a plastic bag in this case) either has these features or it does not. This is what separates attributes from other product descriptions. Attributes are sometimes listed on the products we buy. We usually buy a product because of its features. In fact, one way to list the product attributes is to review its sales literature. As you can imagine, most marketing professionals define products by their features.

Table 7 can be defined as a product specification. In fact, most quality professionals develop such specifications to define the product. A list of product features will generally be more detailed than that given in Table 7.

Attribute specifications can be found in most inspection departments. They are used for visual inspection and product testing. Many functional tests are performed to ensure that product features operate as they should.

Variables

Variables are defined as "measureable product characteristics" that we can measure with test equipment. Examples include the mileage reading on a car's odometer or the amount of milk poured into a measuring cup. Table 8 lists product variables for a plastic bag.

Table 8: Product Variables for a Plastic Bag

Item	Parameter	Nominal	Unit	CR	MA	MI
1	Width	12	Inches ($\pm$)	0.25	0.10	0.05
2	Length	12	Inches ($\pm$)	0.25	0.10	0.05

A product can include any number of variables. As with attributes, each must be ranked according to the level of risk in relation to human needs. With variables, however, it is possible to define how much our manufacturing system will be allowed to vary. In this case, the system can be defined as the manufacturing process. In most cases, variables will be compared with plastic bags produced on a machine. A measurement of the bags produced on a machine and allowance for the variables will indicate how far the machine will vary from the target.

In Table 8, columns are labeled similarly to those for product attributes in Table 7. If the machine produces a product that varies $\pm$ 0.05 inches, this would be considered a minor risk. If a bag is produced that varies $\pm$ 0.25 inches, this would be considered a critical risk and the product rejected.

Table 8 is similar to an engineering specification. Most engineers define products in terms of numbers. The major difference is that quality specifications must reflect real-world needs. Some engineers do not consider the amount of variation that occurs in manufacturing systems. Quality specifications reflect the process variation and customer needs. Conflict between engineering specifications and quality specifications are not unusual because many engineers do not monitor their designs through the mass production process. Thus, they may not understand the relationship between actual customer needs and manufacturability.

Operating Conditions

Operating conditions describe the environment in which the product is intended to operate. In effect, this refers to the state of nature to which the product will be exposed in the course of its normal use and includes shelf life, temperature, and vibration. Table 9 lists operating conditions to which a plastic bag might be exposed.

Table 9: Product Operating Conditions for a Plastic Bag

Item	Condition	Nominal	Unit	CR	MA	MI
1	Life	3	Years	1	2	2.5
2	Low-temperature operation	− 32	Degrees	70	40	31
3	Low-temperature storage	− 40	Degrees	50	30	35

It is important to list as many conditions as possible to which the product might be exposed — from shipping to use. As shown in Table 9, operating conditions are described in the same manner in which variables are written. Here, too, each condition must be associated with the five basic human needs.

Some of these conditions are defined by the engineering group. Usually, however, the engineers do not know how to define the environment, except in the simplest terms. It is up to reliability engineers as part of the quality profession to define these conditions.

Review

External needs are defined by a description of attributes, variables, and operating conditions. Each of these categories is associated with a risk — critical, major, or minor. These descriptions can be used to evaluate a system's success in doing what was required by customers' external needs. The difference is the amount of inefficiency in the system.

Chapter 3
DEFINING THE PROCESS

Another vital step is defining the system used to produce a product (Figure 6). Essentially, we must start with our organization and the production methods used. Our operation must be evaluated from the top down to understand the decisions, methods, and procedures used to make a product. In this chapter, the manner in which a basic manufacturing system is described will be explored.

Organizational Chart

The first step in defining a system is to describe the decision-making responsibility and duties of each person in the system. This is achieved through an organizational chart which depicts the lines of authority and responsibility in a system. A job description of each position accompanies the organizational chart.

Figure 7 shows a typical organizational chart from which the element of each person and major elements of the departments are determined and interdepartmental comparisons are made.

Table 10 is a basic outline for job descriptions that should be attached to the organizational chart. These descriptions are necessary to ensure that proper scope and depth are given to the appropriate people.

Organizational charts help determine the emphasis the company places on various operations. The Quality Department may be part of the Manufacturing Department, which is equivalent to placing the Accounting Department or Personnel Department under Manufacturing. Another interesting facet of organizational charts is the management level of each department. Everyone in the company who reports to the president may be a vice-president, except

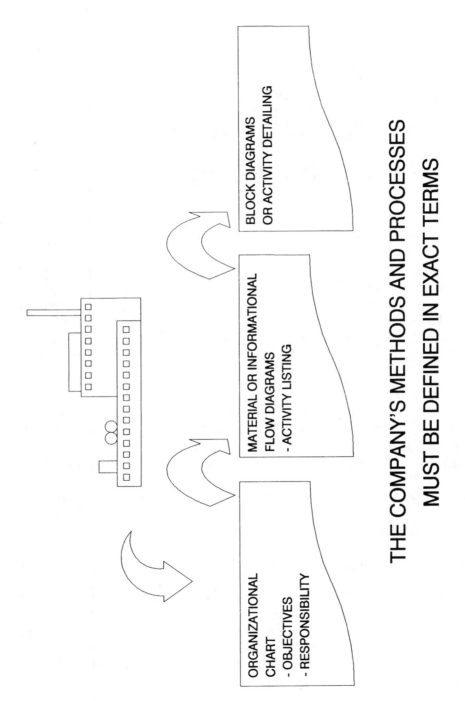

Figure 6: Business processes have three layers: formal organization, material/informational flow, and block diagrams.

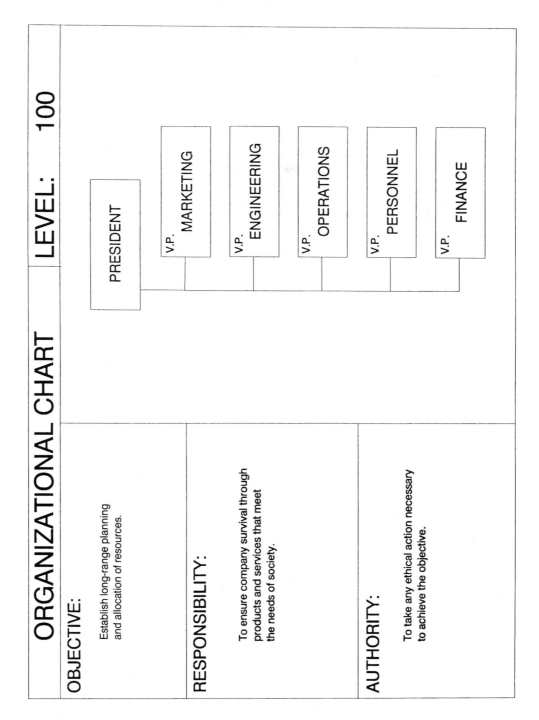

Figure 7: The organizational chart should include the objective, responsibility, and authority of each group defined.

Table 10: Outline for Job Descriptions

Term	Description
Title	Position title
Education	The highest level of education required to fulfill the responsibilities
Experience	The highest amount of experience required for job performance
Job Description	Tasks, duties, activities, and performance standards
Job Specification	Abilities, skills, and traits needed to do the job

for the quality manager. This clearly demonstrates the emphasis the decision makers in the company have assigned to quality.

Organizational charts will help determine the origins of problems and evaluate the system that has been established to determine its efficiency.

Material Flow Diagrams

Another chart that can be used to define a system is a material flow diagram that shows the flow of material throughout the system — from raw materials to finished product. The purpose of this chart is to show material flow rather than inspection points or other operations.

Figure 8 is a simple material flow diagram in which material flows from left to right. On the far left is the fabrication process, which is the first transformation of incoming material. The next process is the assembly process, where pieces produced during fabrication are put together. The final step shown in Figure 8 at the far right is the testing and packaging process. Regardless of what a company produces, it follows these three basic steps.

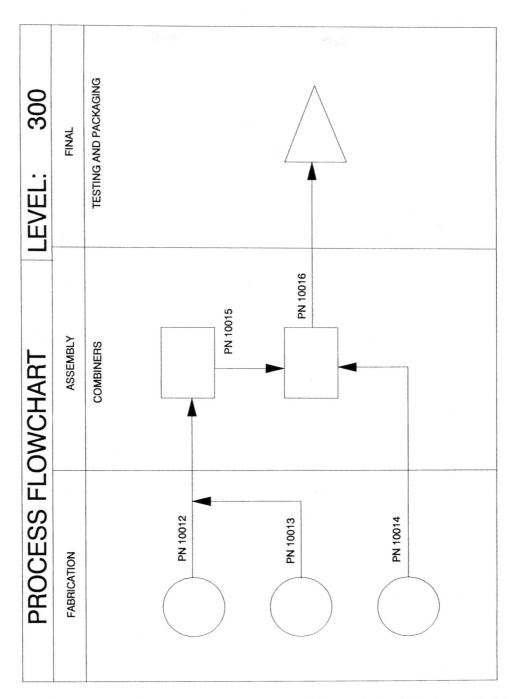

Figure 8: The material flowchart should read from left to right showing how the material is transformed into a final product.

The following standard symbols are used to describe material flow:

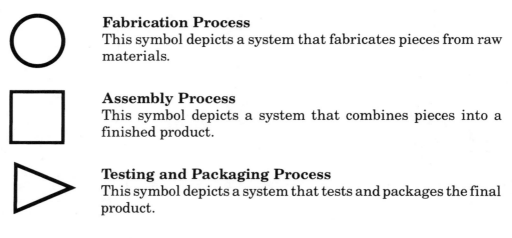

Fabrication Process
This symbol depicts a system that fabricates pieces from raw materials.

Assembly Process
This symbol depicts a system that combines pieces into a finished product.

Testing and Packaging Process
This symbol depicts a system that tests and packages the final product.

As with the organizational chart, a brief description of each of the processes defined in the material flowchart should be included on a separate page. The charts should not be cluttered with descriptions and explanations; these can be included on the attached chart description. If too much information is provided in the chart, it will become unreadable, defeating its purpose. A cursory look at the flowchart should reveal its purpose and the flow of the material through the system. If the reader needs additional detailed information, he or she can refer to the attached description. An easy rule to remember is to "keep it short and simple."

Simplified Block Diagrams

The last step in defining a system is to describe the machines used to fabricate and assemble the final product, which will require machine observation during actual operation. These machines perform redundant operations and make identical parts.

The development of simplified block diagrams of these machines does not require technical knowledge. Nontechnical people should be able to understand in simple terms how these machines operate. To accomplish this, the diagram shows only those parts that actually come in contact with the material used in the part it produces. Again, engineering knowledge is not needed to understand machine operations. In fact, technical people tend to overlook the machine's purpose and view it as a finite technical system devoid of its intended use.

Another reason for simplified block diagrams is that some plant managers may not fully understand how their machines operate. In fact, some engineers may not know how their designs will operate in actual practice. The best

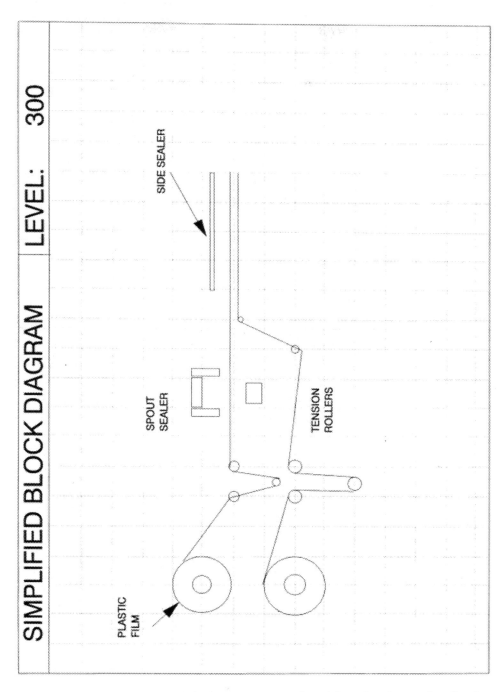

Figure 9: The simplified block diagram should only show the devices impacting or transforming material.

resource is the machine operator who has day-to-day responsibility for its operation. The amount of information a machine operator is able to provide can be astonishing.

Figure 9 shows a simplified block diagram of a machine that makes plastic bags. Only those operations that are critical to the processing of material are shown.

Review

Organizational charts, material flow diagrams, and simplified block diagrams of the machine processes are needed to describe a system. Each of these elements includes attached detailed descriptions for a more complete explanation of each step depicted in the chart or diagram.

Chapter 4
PROBLEM SOLVING

It is a fact of life that problems exist. While some people choose to avoid problems, others actively pursue solving them. Solving a problem, however, is not necessarily enough. Sometimes merely solving a system problem fails to identify its cause. An analogy would be fighting a fire repeatedly without addressing the reason the fire recurs.

It is frustrating to solve a problem only to see it resurface. The purpose of problem solving is to identify the root cause. If the cause is discovered and the problem solved, it is not necessary to find ways to deal with the problem again. This may require alteration of the manner in which a task is performed to make it work better. If the method is not changed, the problem remains. Many companies go out of business because they do not change quickly enough to satisfy their customers' needs.

This chapter will address how to evaluate a problem and direct change. Decision makers must commit to the change; without their commitment, solutions cannot be implemented. This usually happens in companies that are complacent. The result is a poor-quality product.

Problem-Solving Techniques

The problem-solving techniques involve seven steps:

1. Identify the problem
2. Gather data
3. Analyze the data
4. Develop solutions
5. Develop a plan
6. Implement the plan
7. Correct the plan, as necessary

Each step must be performed successfully to solve a problem. Each step is explored in detail below to understand its importance.

Problem Scenario

You are the quality manager of company ABC. It has been brought to your attention by the company owner that one of the machines that produces plastic bags has a 28% defect rate. The last production report showed that 55 of 200 bags were defective. Table 11 lists the defects found by a line inspector.

This defect rate is of major concern because it represents the company's ability to provide a product to a new customer, which will affect a substantial part of the plastic bag market.

Table 11: Defect List

Defect Description	No. Found
Top seal leakers	15
Left seal leakers	4
Spout leakers	9
Pinholes	22
Missing spouts	3
Damaged spouts	1
Open bottom seals	1
TOTAL	**55**

In light of the defects listed in Table 11, it is tempting to concentrate on the defects that have the highest frequencies. First, however, we must identify the problem.

Identification of the Problem

To identify the problem, the list in Table 11 must be organized. To accomplish this, the defects are ranked from the most to the least frequently occurring. This has been done in Table 12.

Table 12: Sorted Defect List

Defect Description	No. Found	%	Sum
Pinholes	22	40	40
Top seal leakers	15	27	67
Spout leakers	9	16	83
Left seal leakers	4	7	90
Missing spout	3	5	95
Damaged spout	1	2	97
Open bottom seal	1	2	99
TOTAL	**55**	0.99	---

Table 12 has two additional columns that do not appear in Table 11 whose values were determined by dividing the quantity of the defects by the total number of defects. For example, to find the percent of pinholes, 22 is divided by 55, which yields 0.40. We then multiply 0.40 by 100 to arrive at the percent. We also added the values in the sum column together. For example, the final value for top seal leakers was found by adding 40 and 27 together, which yields 67.

Ranking the defects yields a better understanding of the problem. This is a vital step in problem identification. All problems exhibit symptoms. The defects listed in Table 12 are the symptoms of the real problem. We must be able to isolate the symptoms that will lead us to the cause of the problem. Ranking the defects has isolated the principal few symptoms.

The next step is to determine which of these defects represent the vital few that need to be investigated. These will be evaluated as a group to obtain a clearer picture.

Example 1
Which defect represents 40% of all defects?

Step 1   Pinholes = 22
Total defects = 55

Step 2   % = Pinholes/total defects
= 22/55
= 0.40
= 0.40 × 100
= 40%

Step 3   40% of the defects are pinholes

Example 2
Which defects represent 83% of all defects?

> *Step 1*   As determined from the % column:
> $$\text{Pinholes} = 0.40$$
> $$\text{Top seal leakers} = 0.27$$
> $$\text{Spout leakers} = 0.16$$

> *Step 2*
> $$\begin{aligned} s\% &= \text{Pin holes} + \text{top seal leakers} + \text{spout leakers} \\ &= 0.40 + 0.27 + 0.16 \\ &= 0.83 \times 100 \\ &= 83\% \end{aligned}$$

> *Step 3*   Pinholes, top seal leakers, and spout leakers represent 83% of all defects

For example 2, Table 12 could have been used to find the value 0.83. Referral to the ranked list for a value between 80% and 95% normally would isolate the critical symptoms. If the cause of the pinholes, top seal leakers, and spout leakers is found, 83% of the defects can be eliminated.

At this point, the problem symptoms can be defined as pinholes, top seal leakers, and spout leakers. The problem has now been defined in a way that will guide toward a useful solution. If this approach is not taken, the real cause of the problem may never be discovered, resulting in symptom recurrence.

Gathering Data

The next step in solving problems is to gather information specific to the vital few symptoms. Do not be distracted from the symptoms you are investigating. If you become diverted from gathering data specifically related to the vital few symptoms, it is possible that fraud may be occurring.

With respect to the symptoms listed in Table 12, the following information was found:

1. Pinholes in the top seal
2. Top seal leakers are caused by pinholes
3. Leaking spouts are caused by pinholes
4. The heating sealer temperature is 450°
5. The temperature of the sealer drifts $\pm 5°$

The information listed is specific to the symptoms under investigation. It cannot be overemphasized that the data collected must be related to the symptoms being researched. The data are otherwise worthless.

Analysis of the Data

Data analysis requires statistical and technical knowledge. To relate the data to a cause requires a scientific understanding of the process. Technical knowledge alone is not enough; an understanding of natural process variation is also essential. This requires a good understanding of statistical methods in a description of states of nature.

Information gathered for the symptoms listed in Table 12 yields a common characteristic. From the information below, it appears that pinholes and temperature are common characteristics of the symptoms.

Developing Solutions

In the preceding step, pinholes and temperature were found to be common to the problem symptoms. For this example, one solution could be easily developed: temperature is the problem that causes all the defects (symptoms) to occur.

Most problem analyses are not this obvious. A problem often has many possible solutions. These solutions can be devised through brainstorming and should be rank ordered according to the number and amount of resources needed to implement them. This will aid in the next step of developing a plan.

Developing a Plan

Based on the solutions, a plan must be established to allocate the required personnel and resources. An action plan calls for a list of the steps needed and should include the length of time necessary to complete each step. Table 13 is an activity list for a plan to solve the problem presented in Table 11.

Table 13: Activity List

Activity	Duration (weeks)	Prerequisites
1. Arrange for test equipment	2.0	0
2. Arrange for staff	1.0	1
3. Allocate machine downtime	2.0	2
4. Perform tests	0.5	3
5. Correction and summary	3.0	4

In Table 13, each activity is listed along with the amount of time required. In addition, prerequisite activities that must be performed before we can proceed to the next step in the plan are listed. The plan can be further developed with a time line chart (Table 14).

Table 14: Time Line Chart

Activity	1	2	3	4	5	6	7	8
1. Test equipment	XXXXXXX							
2. Staff		XXXXXXX						
3. Downtime			XX					
4. Testing				XXXXXXXX				
5. Corrections						XXXXXXXXXXXXXXX		

Table 14 provides a visual representation of the time and steps required to complete the plan. The plan can be dissected further by the amount of time allocated or cost. When a plan is costed out, three elements must be estimated: direct labor costs, direct material costs, and allocated overhead costs.

Direct labor costs are the hourly costs of the employees needed to work on the problem. The hours from the activity list are multiplied by an hourly rate to obtain the dollar amount.

Direct material costs are the costs of equipment rentals and spoilage created by testing. Equipment rental rates are easily determined, but material spoilage must be approximated.

Allocated overhead costs are the fixed costs associated with doing business. They are the expenses a company incurs even if it does not make any money. Examples of allocated overhead costs are rent, utilities, and licensing fees. For the purposes of this discussion, the standard of 65% of the combined direct labor and direct material costs will be used, and it will be assumed that the direct labor cost for this plan is $50,000 and the direct material cost is $10,000. The total cost for direct labor and materials is therefore $60,000 ($50,000 + $10,000). Allocated overhead costs will be $60,000 × 0.65, or $39,000. Therefore, the total cost to implement the plan is $99,000.

Implementing the Plan

To correct the problem, it is important to implement the plan that has been developed. Many solutions have never been found simply because the developed plan was never implemented.

Corrections to the Plan

Because no plan is foolproof, it must be modified if the desired results are not obtained. Many plans have not solved problems because management refused to change the plan when warranted by the outcome. It may be necessary to revise the entire plan and to develop other solutions.

Review

To solve a problem, seven steps must be followed:

1. Identify the problem
2. Gather data
3. Analyze the data
4. Develop solutions
5. Develop a plan
6. Implement the plan
7. Correct the plan, as necessary

Chapter 5
STATISTICAL METHODS

In Chapter 4, temperature was found to be a common element to the symptoms of the problem. This chapter explores the way in which common elements are controlled to prevent defects (symptoms) from occurring. If the common characteristic(s) that causes the defects (symptoms) can be identified, its effects can be limited.

Systems can be controlled indirectly or directly. Indirect control allows the system to operate without intervention, correcting it only when the output produces defects (problem symptoms). This type of control essentially allows defects to occur. Indirect control is the most inefficient control system, both economically and practically. It is equivalent to steering a car only when it goes off the road.

Direct control places self-adjusting measures on common characteristics of the system. The automatic correction of the system when these common characteristics begin to drift into regions that are known to create defects (problem symptoms) enables their prevention. This system of control is the most economical and creates a highly efficient system to meet external needs.

Table 15 shows temperature readings obtained during the planning phase of problem solving.

The heater strives to maintain a constant temperature of 450°. As seen from the measurements in Table 15, this temperature is not maintained. This does not mean that the temperature control is defective. A natural variation occurs when any system strives to maintain an exact value. This variation occurs in nature as well. No two things produced are ever exactly the same. No two flowers are exactly alike. No two trees are exactly alike. Because no two similar items can ever be exactly the same, the differences between them must be understood.

Table 15: Raw Temperature Measurements

450°	446°	453°	446°	441°	451°
445°	448°	451°	450°	450°	452°
445°	450°	452°	450°	451°	449°
452°	450°	452°	453°	450°	454°
451°	449°	452°	455°	450°	450°

Measures of Location

Average: Similar items naturally tend to group around a common characteristic. In the case of the temperature readings in Table 15, the values are expected to be grouped around the 450° reading. One way to determine the central tendency of the values is to find the average value. This is done by adding all the readings together and dividing by the total number of values, as shown in example 1 below.

Example 1
The sum of all the readings in Table 15 = 13,513

$$\text{Number of readings} = 30$$
$$\text{Average} = 13,513/30$$
$$= 450.43$$

In example 1, the central tendency of the temperature readings is calculated. Remember that the system is striving to maintain a constant temperature of 450°. Because no two values can be identical, this average is the value around which the individual readings group.

Median: Another measure of central tendency is called the median. This is a value that resides between the highest and lowest readings. To find the median, the temperature readings must be rank ordered (Table 16).

The highest and lowest values in Table 16 are easily found. Example 2 below shows how the median value of the temperature readings is calculated.

Example 2
Count off an equal number of measurements from the high and low end of the series of readings until the center value is reached. In this case, there is an even number of readings. Therefore, the average of the two center readings is used to calculate the median.

$$\text{Median} = (450° + 450°)/2$$
$$= 900°/2$$
$$= 450°$$

Table 16: Rank-Ordered Temperature Readings

455°	452°	451°	450°	450°	448°
455°	452°	451°	450°	450°	446°
454°	452°	451°	450°	450°	446°
453°	452°	451°	450°	449°	446°
453°	452°	450°	450°	449°	445°

Mode: Still another measure of central tendency is called the mode. The mode is simply the most frequently occurring value. Table 17 shows the frequency of the temperature readings listed in Table 16.

Table 17: Temperature Reading Frequency

Temperature Reading	Frequency
455°	2
454°	1
453°	2
452°	5
451°	4
450°	9
449°	2
448°	1
446°	3
445°	1

As seen in Table 17, the value 455° occurs twice. The most frequently occurring value is the temperature reading 450°. Because the mode is the most frequently occurring value, 450° is the mode value.

In some cases, several values have the highest frequency. In such cases, readings are said to have a multimodal central tendency.

Even when a system strives to produce identical items, no two items are exactly the same. The unit-to-unit differences tend to group around a central value that can be determined by finding the average, the median, and the mode values.

Measures of Variation

Once the central tendency of the temperature readings is determined, the next step is to determine how far the individual values range from that value, or the amount of variation from the central tendency value (the spread of the values away from the central value).

Range: One method to determine the spread of the readings is to find the range. The range is found by subtracting the highest value from the lowest value, which will reveal how many readings lie between the highest and lowest values. The range is calculated in example 3.

Example 3
Range = Highest reading − lowest reading
Range = 455 − 445
      = 10

Example 3 shows that the range of values in Table 16 is 10, which means that there is a spread of 10 whole-number values between the highest and lowest temperature readings of 455° and 445°.

Variance: Another measurement of variation is known as the variance, which is calculated by subtracting the average from each individual reading, squaring the difference, summing the differences, and dividing the sum by the number of readings minus one. Table 18 is a partial list of the temperature readings and shows how the variance is calculated.

Table 18 shows the sum of the squared differences to be 180. To obtain the variance from this number, 180 is simply divided by 29 (the number of readings minus one, i.e., 30 − 1), or 6.207. This means that the average distance of our readings from the average (central tendency) value is 6.207. In other words, the temperature readings will fall 6.207° above or below the average reading of 450°. To prove this, 6.207° is subtracted from and added to the average value. This yields 443.793° and 456.206°. Table 16 shows that all the temperature readings fall between those numbers.

Standard Deviation: Another way to determine the spread of values is to find the standard deviation, a value that divides the spread of the readings into measured units from the central tendency. The standard deviation is the square root of the variance (the square root of the variance 6.207 is 2.491). Sixty-eight percent of temperature readings fall within one standard deviation above or below the average value. Simply put, 68% of the readings will be between 447.059° and 452.941°. In fact, 86% of the readings will fall between two standard deviations (2×2.941) of the central tendency, or from 444.118° to 455.882°. Furthermore, 99.86% of the readings will be within three standard deviations (3×2.941) of the central tendency, or from 441.177° to 458.823°.

In summary, there are three measures of the spread of readings from the

Table 18: Temperature Reading Variables

Reading	Average	Difference	Squared Difference
455°	450°	5	25
455°	450°	5	25
454°	450°	4	16
453°	450°	3	9
453°	450°	3	9
•	•	•	•
•	•	•	•
•	•	•	•
445°	450°	−5	25
TOTALS	---	---	**180**

average temperature value (central tendency). These measures of spread (variation) are the range, the variance, and the standard deviation. These values provide a means to determine how far the individual values are from the average value and indicate how much each unit can vary from the central tendency.

In the case of the temperature readings, the distance the temperature will drift from the desired setting of 450° can be determined. This is very useful for system control. If system variation (drifts) can be controlled, its efficiency can be increased, thereby preventing defects (problem symptoms). The system thus will not create spoilage or scrap caused by inefficiency.

Control Charts

Systems can be controlled directly by monitoring their common characteristics via control charts. Control charts monitor key characteristics of the system so that adjustments can be made to prevent defects (problem symptoms).

One type of control chart, known as the average and range chart, tracks the average value and range over time. To construct this chart, the limits at which adjustments must be made need to be defined. To do this, the average value (central tendency) must be found. Because all possible readings cannot be obtained from any system, a sample must be obtained. This sample must include 30 or more values to ensure that there is an equal number of values above and below the average (this is described by the central limit theorem).

The constants listed in Table 19 are used to calculate the control limits. Remember that the control limits will dictate when adjustments must be made to the system to maintain efficient operation. When the system operates within its limits, it is said to be in a state of control.

Table 19: Control Limit Constants

Sample Size	Average A_2	D_3	Range D_4
2	1.88	0	3.27
3	1.02	0	2.57
4	0.73	0	2.28
5	0.58	0	2.11

Table 19 shows constants that can be used to determine control limits for sample averages and ranges. Because more than one reading at a time will be obtained, Table 19 shows constants for different sample sizes. Obviously, it would not be practical to obtain 30 readings each time the system is measured. Most control charts employ a sample size of five readings.

How often should system measurements be obtained? This depends on how much the system varies over time. Most measurements are performed every hour; however, it must be determined how often the system drifts over time, and measurements must be made accordingly.

The following examples show how to calculate control limits with the use of temperature readings on control chart Cl.

CONTROL CHART

No. 100

PRODUCT:	Bag		PART NUMBER:	n001
TOLERANCE:	450 ± 5.8		MACHINE: 1	BY: PDM

DATE	5-1	5-1	5-1	5-1	5-1
TIME	9:00	9:30	10:00	10:30	11:00
READINGS 1	450	446	453	446	451
2	445	448	451	450	452
3	455	450	452	450	449
4	452	450	452	453	454
5	451	449	452	455	450
SUM	2253	2243	2260	2254	2256
AVERAGE	450	449	452	451	451
RANGE	10	4	2	9	5

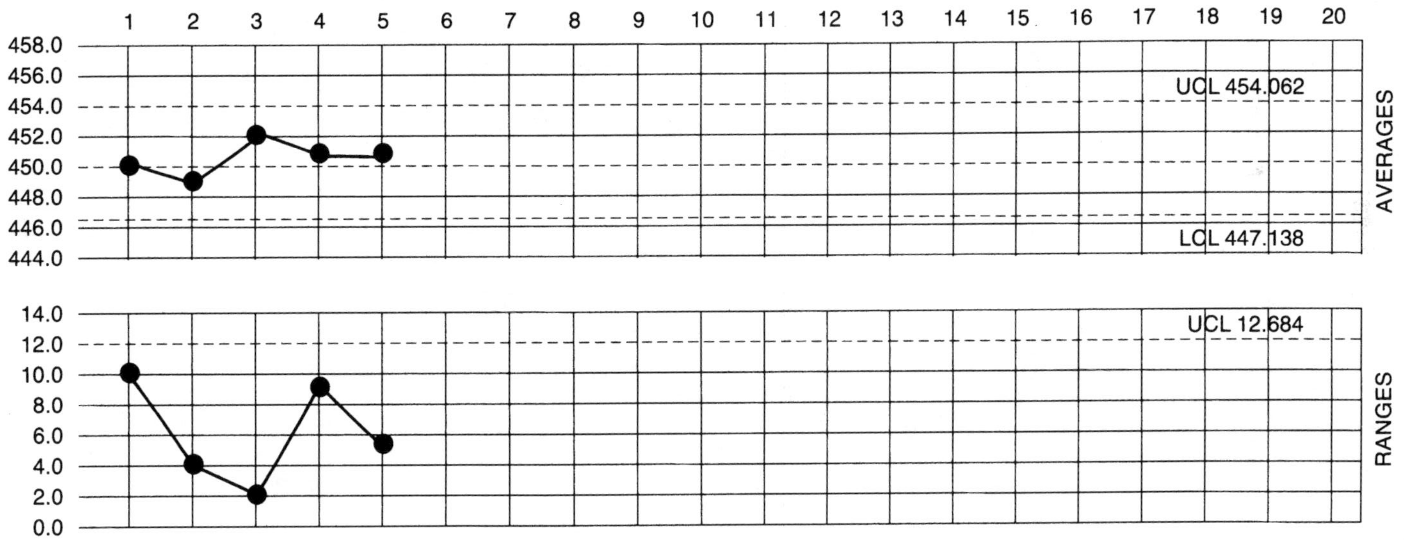

AVERAGES

UCL 454.062

LCL 447.138

RANGES

UCL 12.684

Chart C1

Control Limits for Sample Averages

The following can be determined from control chart C1:

Upper control limit

Average range value = Sum of the sample ranges divided by the
number of samples
= (10+4+2+9+5)/5
= 30/5
= 6

Grand average value = Sum of the sample averages divided by the
number of samples
= (450+119+452+451+451)/5
= 2,253/5
= 450.6 (rounded down to 450)

Upper control limit = Grand average value + (A_2 × average range
value)
= 450 + (0.58 × 6)
= 450 + 3.48
= 453.48

Lower control limit = Average value − (A_2 × average range value)
= 450 − (0.58 × 6)
= 450 − 3.48
= 446.52

These limits dictate when adjustments must be made to the system. In the case of the temperature measurements, the limits indicate when to adjust the temperature back to the average value.

The variation of the system must also be monitored to ensure that the spread of the readings does not become too large. The following examples show how to calculate the control limits for range values.

Control Limits for Sample Ranges

Average range value = Sum of the sample ranges divided by the
number of samples
= (10+4+2+9+5)/5
= 30/5
= 6

Upper control limit = D_4 × average range value
= 2.11 × 6
= 12.66

Lower control limit $= D_3 \times$ average range value
$$= 0 \times 6$$
$$= 0$$

The control limits for sample ranges indicate when adjustments must be made to the system. Each of the control limit calculations employed the constants found in Table 19. The control limits are used to check sample-to-sample averages and ranges. If a sample average goes beyond these control limits, an adjustment must be made to the system. Chart C1 is a control chart for the temperature readings.

Control charts are only a stopgap method to control a system. A more effective means to improve efficiency is to redesign or change the system to eliminate the cause of the problem. This requires the allocation of resources to constantly improve the system. In the case of a temperature problem, it would be efficient to incorporate a temperature control to limit the drift (variation), which would eliminate the need for a control chart.

Control charts should be used only when it is not possible to improve or change the system. It is important to remember that measurements should be made based on the system, *not on its output.* Measurement of the parts made by the system does not constitute direct control. Indirect control allows for defects (problem symptoms) to occur before adjustments are made, while direct control allows adjustments before defects (symptoms) occur. Of course, output and control limits must be compared to determine whether the symptoms have been eliminated, but this is done before the limits are established. The system's output should be checked periodically only to ensure that control remains effective.

Instructions for Control Chart Preparation

For the purpose of these instructions, please refer to the Appendix for control chart constants. Each chart has its own set of constants used to calculate control limits. Refer to the appropriate table in the Appendix for each chart (i.e., Average and Range, Average and Standard Deviation, Median and Range, and Individual and Range).

Variable Control Charts

Average and Range Chart: To prepare a control chart for averages and ranges, follow the steps listed below (also see Chart C1):

Step 1: *Select sample size and frequency*
Select an appropriate sample size and determine how often system measurements are to be made. The object is to obtain enough samples at appropriate times to observe the process variation. Observation of the variation dictates when adjustments need to be made to the system.

Step 2: Take reading
Take readings and annotate them on the chart.

Step 3: Calculate the average and range
As each sample is obtained, individual averages and ranges must be calculated.

Step 4: Scale graph and plot values
After at least 20 samples are obtained, construct the scales for the X and R graphs. Once this has been completed, plot the sample averages and ranges on their prospective graphs.

Step 5: Calculate center line and control limits
After enough samples are obtained (usually 20 or more) calculate their central tendency by taking the average of the sample averages and ranges, as follows:

$$R' = R1 + R2 + R3.../k$$
$$X' = X1 + X2 + X3.../k$$

Where: R1, R2, R3   = Sample ranges
                X1, X2, X3   = Sample averages
                       k   = Number of samples obtained

Calculate the control limits for the averages and range as follows:

Average limits
Upper control limit = $X' + (A2 \times R')$
Lower control limit = $X' - (A2 \times R')$

Range limits
Upper control limit = $D4 \times R'$
Lower control limit = $D3 \times R'$

Where: A2, D3, D4 are constants (see the Appendix)

Note: The prime symbol "'" (i.e., R', X') is used to denote average in this text.

Average and Standard Deviation Chart: To prepare a control chart for averages and standard deviations, follow the steps listed below (also see Chart C2):

Step 1: Select sample size and frequency
Select an appropriate sample size and determine how often system measurements are to be made. The object is to obtain enough samples at appropriate times to observe the process variation. Observation of the variation dictates when adjustments need to be made to the system.

CONTROL CHART

PRODUCT:	Bag		PART NUMBER:	n001		No. 100
TOLERANCE:	450 ± 5.8		MACHINE:	1	BY: PDM	

DATE		5-1	5-1	5-1	5-1	5-1
TIME		9:00	9:30	10:00	10:30	11:00
READINGS	1	450	446	453	446	451
	2	445	448	451	450	452
	3	455	450	452	450	449
	4	452	450	452	453	454
	5	451	449	452	455	450
SUM		2253	2243	2260	2254	2256
AVERAGE		450	449	452	451	451
S.D.		3.6	1.7	0.7	3.4	1.9

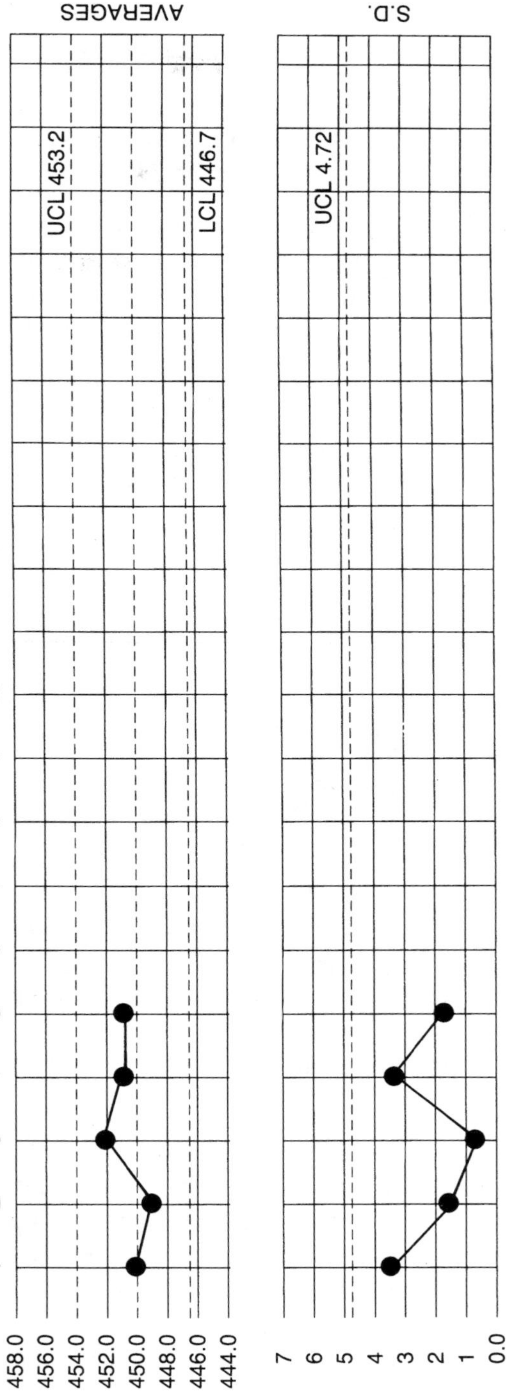

AVERAGES — UCL 453.2, LCL 446.7

S.D. — UCL 4.72

Chart C2

Step 2: Take readings
Take readings and annotate them on the chart.

Step 3: Calculate the average and standard deviation
As each sample is obtained, individual averages and standard deviations must be calculated.

Step 4: Scale graph and plot values
After at least 20 samples are obtained, construct the scales for the X and S graphs. Once this has been completed, plot the sample averages and standard deviations on their prospective graphs.

Step 5: Calculate center line and control limits
After enough samples are obtained, which results in a total of 100 individual readings, calculate their central tendency by taking the average of the sample averages and standard deviations, as follows:

$$X^I = X1 + X2 + X3 \ldots /k$$
$$S^I = S1 + S2 + S3 \ldots /k$$

Where: S1, S2, S3 = Sample standard deviations
X1, X2, X3 = Sample averages
k = Number of samples obtained

Calculate the control limits for the averages and ranges as follows:

Average limits
Upper control limit = $X^I + (A3 \times S^I)$
Lower control limit = $X^I - (A3 \times S^I)$

Standard deviation limits
Upper control limit = $B4 \times S^I$
Lower control limit = $B3 \times S^I$

Where: A3, B3, B4 are constants (see the Appendix)

Median and Range Chart: To prepare a control chart for medians and ranges follow the steps listed below (also see Chart C3):

Step 1: Select sample size and frequency
Select an appropriate sample size and determine how often system measurements are to be made. The object is to obtain enough samples at appropriate times to observe the process variation. Observation of the variation dictates when adjustments must be made to the system.

Step 2: Take readings
Take readings and annotate them on the chart.

CONTROL CHART

No. 100

PRODUCT:	Bag	PART NUMBER:	n001
TOLERANCE:	450 ± 5.8	MACHINE: 1	BY: PDM

DATE		5-1	5-1	5-1	5-1	5-1
TIME		9:00	9:30	10:00	10:30	11:00
READINGS	1	450	446	453	446	451
	2	445	448	451	450	452
	3	455	450	452	450	449
	4	452	450	452	453	454
	5	451	449	452	455	450
SUM						
MEDIAN		451	449	452	450	451
RANGE		10	4	2	9	5

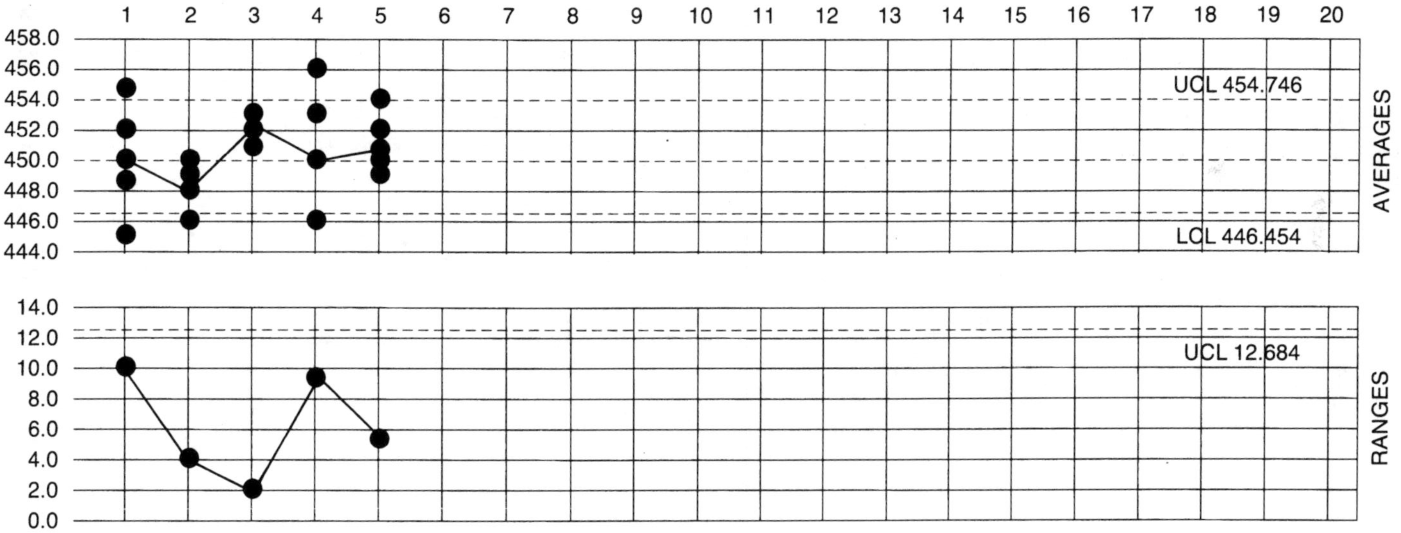

AVERAGES

UCL 454.746

LCL 446.454

RANGES

UCL 12.684

Chart C3

Step 3: Calculate the average and standard deviation
As each sample is obtained, their individual medians and ranges must be calculated.

Step 4: Scale graph and plot values
After at least 20 samples are obtained, construct the scales for the median and range graphs. Once this has been completed, plot the individual readings per sample and ranges on their prospective graphs.

Step 5: Calculate center line and control limits
After enough samples are obtained, which results in a total of 100 individual readings, calculate their central tendency by taking the average of the sample medians and ranges as follows:

$$R^l = R1 + R2 + R3 \ldots /k$$
$$M^l = M1 + M2 + M3 \ldots /k$$

Where: M1, M2, M3 = Sample medians
             R1, R2, R3 = Sample ranges
                   k = Number of samples obtained

Calculate the control limits for the averages and ranges as follows:

Average limits
Upper control limit = $M^l + (A4 \times R^l)$
Lower control limit = $M^l - (A4 \times R^l)$

Range limits
Upper control limit = $D4 \times R^l$
Lower control limit = $D3 \times R^l$

Where: A2, D3, D4 are constants (see the Appendix)

Individuals and Moving Range Chart: To prepare a chart for individuals and moving range, follow the steps listed below (also see Chart C4):

Step 1: Select sample size and frequency
Select an appropriate sample size for ranges and determine how often system measurements are to be made. The object is to obtain enough samples at appropriate times to observe the process variation. Observation of the variation dictates when adjustments must be made to the system.

Step 2: Take readings
Take readings and annotate them on the chart.

Step 3: Calculate the average and standard deviation
As each sample is taken we must calculate the range. This step differs from that of the other charts in the calculation of the range between

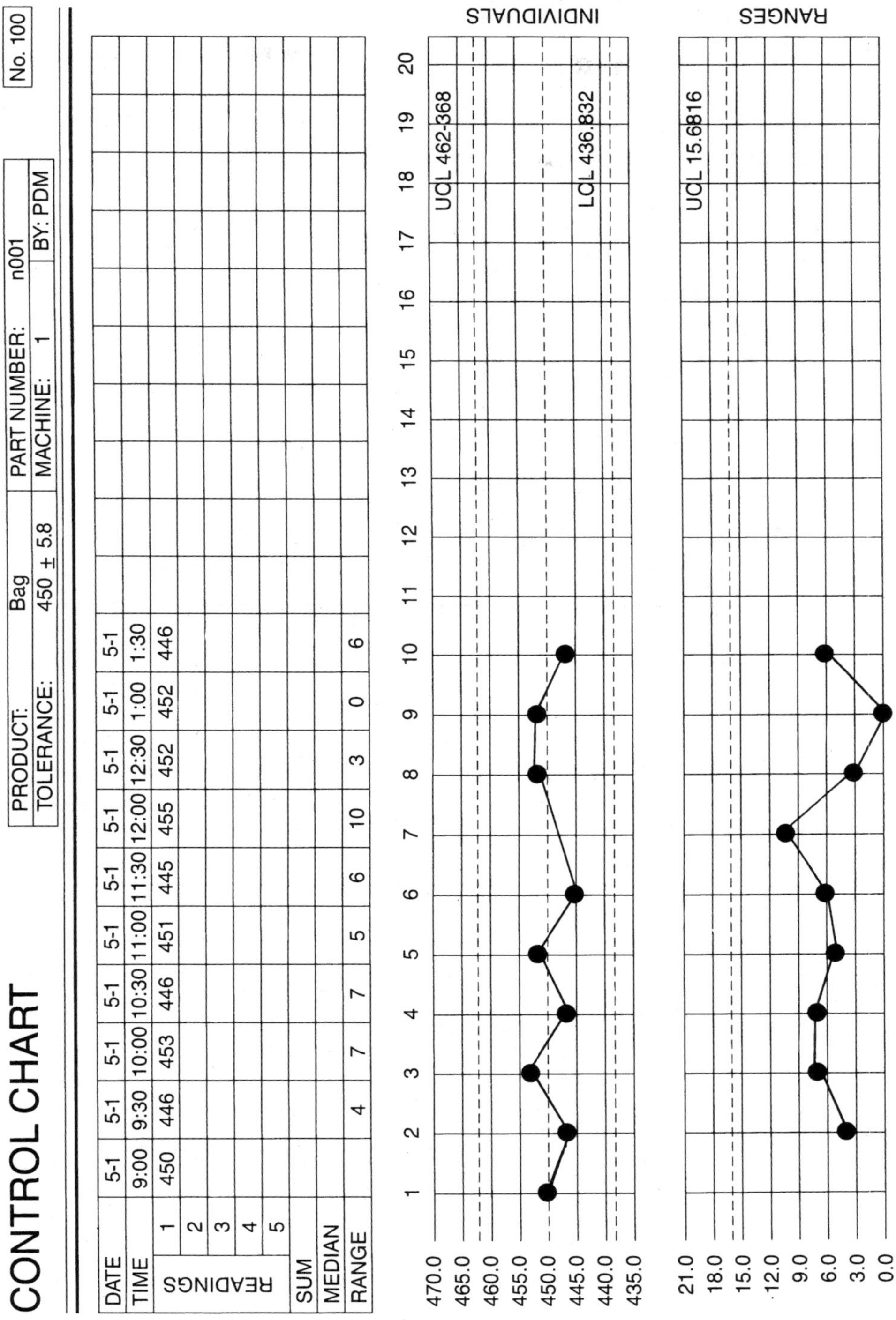

CONTROL CHART

No. 100

| PRODUCT: | Bag | PART NUMBER: | n001 |
| TOLERANCE: | 450 ± 5.8 | MACHINE: 1 | BY: PDM |

DATE	5-1	5-1	5-1	5-1	5-1	5-1	5-1	5-1	5-1	5-1
TIME	9:00	9:30	10:00	10:30	11:00	11:30	12:00	12:30	1:00	1:30
READINGS 1	450	446	453	446	451	445	455	452	452	446
2										
3										
4										
5										
SUM										
MEDIAN										
RANGE		4	7	7	5	6	10	3	0	6

INDIVIDUALS

UCL 462.368

LCL 436.832

RANGES

UCL 15.6816

Chart C4

samples. The number of values used to determine the range becomes our sample size.

Step 4:   *Scale graph and plot values*
After at least 20 samples are obtained, construct the scales for the graphs. Once this has been completed, plot the individual values and moving range on their prospective graphs.

Step 5:   *Calculate center line and control limits*
After enough samples are obtained, which results in a total of 100 individual readings, calculate their central tendency by taking the average of the sample averages and ranges as follows:

$$X' = X1 + X2 + X3 \ldots /k$$
$$R' = R1 + R2 + R3 \ldots /k$$

Where: R1, R2, R3 = Sample range
            X1, X2, X3 = Sample value
                    k = Number of samples obtained

Calculate the control limits for the averages and ranges as follows:
   Average limits
   Upper control limit = $X' + (E2 \times R')$
   Lower control limit = $X' - (E2 \times R')$

   Range limits
   Upper control limit = $D4 \times R'$
   Lower control limit = $D3 \times R'$

Where: E2, D3, D4 are constants (see the Appendix)

Attribute Control Charts

Sometimes it is helpful to track attribute data. The control charts described below are used to perform trend tracking of attribute data. These charts are used similarly to variable control charts, i.e., to detect abnormal conditions and correct the system.

There are four attribute control charts: (1) p' chart for tracking the proportion of nonconforming units, from varying or constant sample sizes; (2) np' chart for tracking the number of nonconforming units, from a constant sample size; (3) c' chart for tracking the number of nonconformities, from a constant sample size; and (4) u' chart for tracking the number of nonconformities per unit, from constant sample sizes. The preparation for each of these charts is described beginning on page 51.

p' *Chart:* To prepare a control chart for the percent of nonconforming units, follow the steps below (also see Chart P1):

Step 1: *Select sample size and frequency*
Select an appropriate sample size and determine how often system measurements are to be made. The object is to obtain enough samples at appropriate times to observe any system variation. Observation of the variation dictates when adjustments must be made to the system.

Step 2: *Make observations/inspections*
Inspect samples and annotate the sample size and number of nonconforming units on the chart.

Step 3: *Calculate the percent of nonconforming units*
This step differs from the variable control charts by the calculation of the ratio between nonconforming units over the number of units in the samples:

$$P = np/n$$

Where:
P = Ratio of nonconforming units
np = Number of nonconforming units
(*Note:* This is shown as "r" on Chart P1.)
n = Sample size
(*Note:* This is shown as "N" on Chart P1.)

Step 4: *Scale graph and plot values*
After at least 20 samples are obtained, construct the scales for the graph. Once this has been completed, plot the percentage values.

Step 5: *Calculate center line and control limits*
After enough samples are obtained, calculate their central tendency by taking the average of the sample percentages as follows:

$$p' = np1+np2+np3...+npk/n1+n2+n3...+nk$$

Where: $np1, np2, np3... = $ Number of nonconforming units
$n1, n2, n3... = $ Sample sizes
$p'... = $ Grand average percent

Calculate the control limits for the sample percentages as follows:

$$\text{Upper control limit} = p' + 3\sqrt{p'(1-p')/n'}$$
$$\text{Lower control limit} = p' - 3\sqrt{p'(1-p')/n'}$$

Where: p' = Grand average percent

n' = Average sample size

Note: Average sample size is denoted as n' and is calculated as follows: $n1+n2+n3\ldots nk$/number of samples.

np' Chart: To prepare a control chart for the number of nonconforming units, follow the steps below:

Step 1: *Select sample size and frequency*

Select an appropriate sample size and determine how often system measurements are to be made. The object is to obtain enough samples at appropriate times to observe any system variation. Observation of the variation indicates when adjustments must be made to the system.

Step 2: *Make observations/inspections*

Inspect the samples and annotate the sample size and the number of nonconforming units on the chart.

Step 3: *Scale graph and plot units*

After at least 20 samples are obtained, construct the scales for the graph. Once this has been completed, plot the number of nonconforming units found in the sample.

Step 4: *Calculate center line and control limits*

After enough samples are obtained, calculate their central tendency by dividing the total number of nonconforming units by the standard sample size, as follows:

$$np' = np1+np2+np3\ldots+npk/k$$

Where: np1, np2, np3 = Number of nonconforming units per subgroup

k = Subgroups

np' = Grand average of nonconforming units

Calculate the control limits for the sample percentages as follows:

$$\text{Upper control limit} = np' + 3\sqrt{np'(1-np')/n'}$$
$$\text{Lower control limit} = np' - 3\sqrt{np'(1-np')/n'}$$

Where: np' = Grand average of nonconforming units

n' = Subgroup size

Note: Average subgroup size is denoted as n' and calculated as follows: $n1+n2+n3\ldots nk$/number of samples.

CONTROL CHART

PRODUCT:			Bag		PART NUMBER:	n001	
SELECT: (P)' NP' C' U'					DEPART.: fab	BY: PDM	No. 100

DATE	1-5	1-6	1-7	1-8	1-9	1-12	1-13			
ID										
N	100	110	101	105	100	100	105			
r	3	1	2	3	0	1	2			
r/N	.03	.009	.019	.028	0	.01	.019			

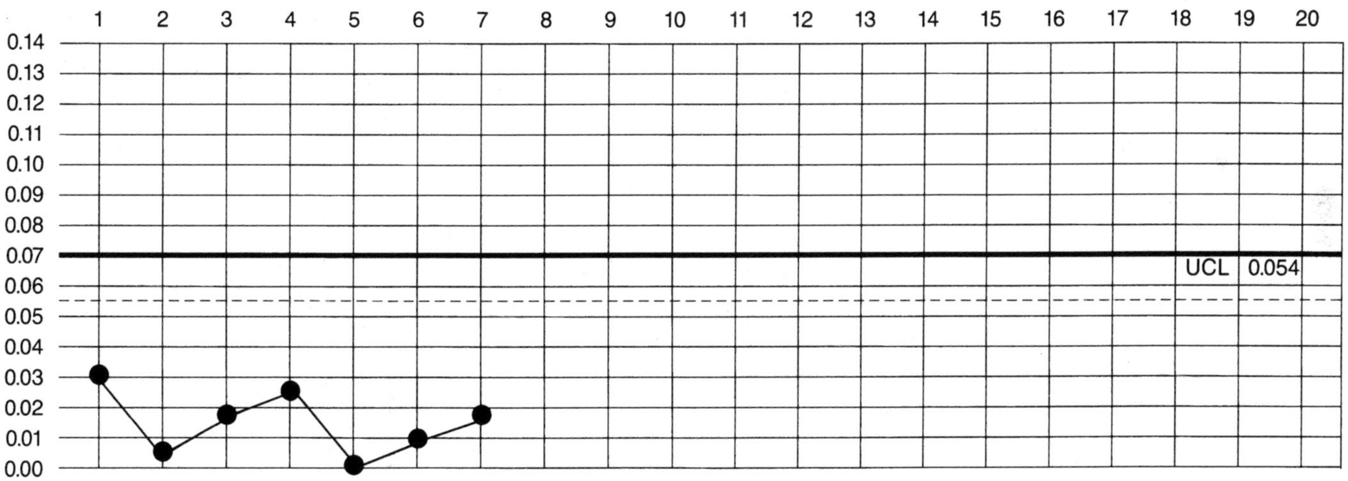

Chart P1

CONTROL CHART

| PRODUCT: | Bag | PART NUMBER: | n001 |
| SELECT: P' (N)P' C' U' | | DEPART.: fab | BY: PDM |

No. 100

DATE	1-5	1-6	1-7	1-8	1-9	1-12	1-13
ID							
N	100	100	100	100	100	100	100
r	3	1	2	3	0	1	2
r/N							

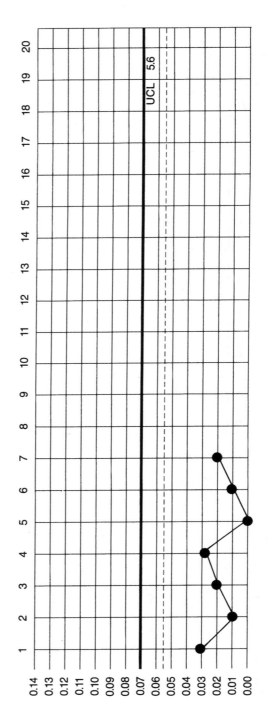

Chart P2

c' *Chart:* To prepare a control chart for the number of nonconformities, follow the steps below (also see Chart P3):

Step 1: *Select sample frequency*
Select a sample size for this chart and determine how often system measurements are to be made. The object is to obtain samples at appropriate times to observe any system variation. Observation of the variation allows detection of when corrective action is needed.

Step 2: *Make observations/inspections*
Inspect the samples and annotate the sample size and number of nonconformities on the chart.

Step 3: *Scale graph and plot units*
After at least 20 samples are obtained, construct the scales for the graph. Once this has been completed, plot the number of nonconformities found in the sample.

Step 4: *Calculate center line and control limits*
After enough samples are obtained, calculate their central tendency by dividing the total number of nonconformities by the number of samples obtained, as follows:

$c' = c1+c2+c3\ldots+ck/k$

Where: c1, c2, c3= Number of nonconformities per subgroup
k= Subgroups
c'= Grand average of nonconformities per unit

Calculate the control limits for the sample nonconformities, as follows:

$$\text{Upper control limit} = c' + 3\sqrt{c'}$$
$$\text{Lower control limit} = c' - 3\sqrt{c'}$$

Where: c' = Grand average of nonconformities per unit

CONTROL CHART

PRODUCT:	Bag	PART NUMBER:	n001	No. 100
SELECT: P' NP' Ⓒ U'		DEPART.: fab	BY: PDM	

DATE									
ID		1-5	1-6	1-7	1-8	1-9			
N		1	1	1	1	1			
r		9	4	5	9	7			
r/N									

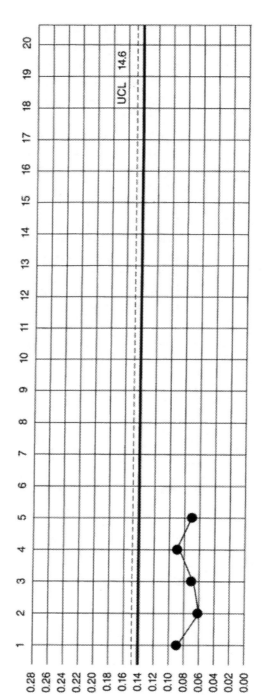

Chart P3

u' Chart: To prepare a control chart for the number of nonconformities, follow the steps below (also see Chart P3):

Step 1: *Select sample frequency*
Select a sample size for this chart and determine how often system measurements are to be made. The object is to obtain samples at appropriate times to observe any system variation. Observation of the variation allows detection of when corrective action is needed.

Step 2: *Make observations/inspections*
Inspect the samples and annotate the number of nonconformities and sample size on the chart.

Step 3: *Scale graph and plot units*
After at least 20 samples are obtained, construct the scales for the graph. Once this has been completed, plot the number of nonconformities found in the sample.

Step 4: *Calculate center line and control limits*
After enough samples are obtained, calculate their central tendency by dividing the total number of nonconformities by the number of samples obtained, as follows:

$$u' = c1+c2+c3 \ldots +ck/n1 + n2 + n3 \ldots +nk$$

Where: c1, c2, c3 = Number of nonconformities per subgroup
k = Subgroup size
u' = Grand average of nonconformities

Calculate the control limits for the sample nonconformities, as follows:

$$\text{Upper control limit} = u' + 3\sqrt{u'/n'}$$
$$\text{Lower control limit} = u' - 3\sqrt{u'/n'}$$

Where: u' = Grand average of nonconformities
n' = Average sample size

CONTROL CHART

| PRODUCT: | Bag |
| SELECT: P' NP' C' U' | |

PART NUMBER:	n001
DEPART.:	fab
	BY: PDM

No. 100

DATE					
ID	1-5	1-6	1-7	1-8	1-9
N	3	3	4	3	5
r	9	4	5	9	7
r/N	3	1.3	1.3	3	1.4

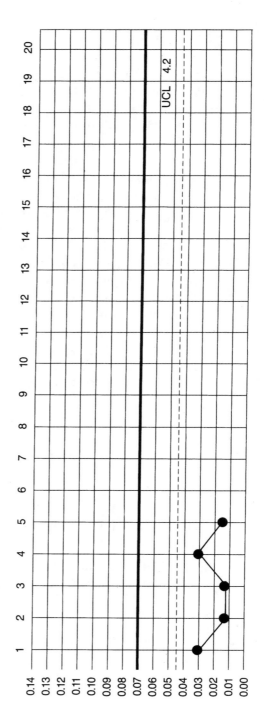

Chart P4

Analysis of Control Charts

The use of control charts requires care in the interpretation of trend in the plotted data. The following conditions indicate that changes must be made to the system.

1. *Points above and below the control limits:* When points are observed above or below the upper or lower control limits, action must be taken to restore control. In the example of the temperature readings, this would require adjustment of the heater temperature.

2. *Long runs above or below the central line:* Seven or more consecutive points above or below the center line indicate a need for action. This might occur if an operator were to constantly adjust the system during a shift.

3. *Points fall close to the control limits or central line:* Points will tend to crowd the control limits if there is an error in their calculation. Control limits should be recalculated.

4. *Points show an upward or downward trend:* When the points on the chart begin to show a trend, something clearly is wrong. The points on a control chart should be random. Therefore, the emergence of a pattern can be attributed to something in the system.

APPENDIX

Table of constants for control charts

Average and Range Chart

Sample Size	A2	d2	D3	D4
2	1.880	1.128	0	3.267
3	1.023	1.693	0	2.574
4	0.7829	2.059	0	2.282
5	0.577	2.326	0	2.114

Average and Standard Deviation Chart

Sample Size	A3	C4	B3	B4
2	2.659	0.7979	0	3.267
3	1.954	0.8862	0	2.568
4	1.628	0.9213	0	2.266
5	1.427	0.9400	0	2.089

Median and Range Chart

Sample Size	A4	d2	D3	D4
2	1.880	1.128	0	3.267
3	1.187	1.693	0	2.574
4	0.796	2.059	0	2.282
5	0.691	2.326	0	2.114

Individual and Range Chart

Sample Size	E2	d2	D3	D4
2	2.660	1.128	0	3.267
3	1.772	1.693	0	2.574
4	1.457	2.059	0	2.282
5	1.290	2.326	0	2.114

Index

A
Action plan, 31-32
Allocated overhead costs, 32
Assembly process, standard symbol
  for, 24
Attribute(s), 15-16
  definition of, 13
Attribute control charts, 50-59
  c' chart, 50, 56, 57
  np' chart, 50, 54, 55
  p' chart, 50, 51-52, 53
  u' chart, 50, 58, 59
Average, 36
  control limits for sample, 42
Average and range chart, 39-40
  sample, 41
  steps in preparing, 43-44
  table of constants for, 61
Average and standard deviation
  chart, 44
  sample, 45
  steps in preparing, 44-46
  table of constants for, 61
Average range value, 42

B
Block diagrams, simplified, 24-26
Brainstorming, 31
Business, applications of quality in,
  4-5

Business modeling, 5, 8
  inputs, 5-6
  transformation process, 6-8
Business system performance, 2
  impact of company organization
    on, 2-4

C
c' chart, 50
  sample, 57
  steps in preparing, 56
Central tendency, 39
Central tendency measures, 36
  average, 36
  median, 36
  mode, 37
Central tendency value, 38
Company organization, impact of,
  on business system performance,
  2-4
Control charts, 39-61
  analysis, 60
  attribute, 50-59
  average and range charts, 39-40
  individual and moving range
    chart, 48-50
  instructions for preparing, 43-44
  table of constants for, 61
Control limit constants, 40-43
Control limits, 40

for sample averages, 42
for sample ranges, 42-43
Critical risk, definition of, 13

D
Data
analysis, 31
gathering, 30
Decision makers, 2, 3, 4, 5
Defect rate, 28
Defects, ranking, 29-30
Direct control, 35, 43
Direct costs
for labor, 32
for material, 32

E
Efficiency, 10
Environment, 6
External needs, 10, 18

F
Fabrication process, standard
symbol for, 24
Financial performance indicators, 1
Financial reports, problems with,
2, 4
Formal organization, 8

G
Grand average value, 42

H
History, 6

I
Indirect control, 35, 43
Individual and moving range chart
sample, 49
steps in preparing, 48, 50
table of constants for, 61
Informal organization, 8

Inputs, 5-6, 8
Internal analyzers, 2, 3, 4, 5

J
Job description, 19
outline for, 22

L
Lower control limit, 42, 43

M
Major risk, definition of, 13
Material flow diagrams, 22-24
Median, 36
Median and range chart, 46
sample, 47
steps in preparing, 46, 48
table of constants for, 61
Minor risk, definition of, 13
Mission, 12
Mode, 37

N
Natural variation, 35
n' chart, 50
sample, 55
steps in preparing, 54

O
Operating conditions, 17
definition of 13,
Organizational chart, 19-22
Organizational model, 8
Outputs, 8

P
p' chart, 50
sample, 53
steps in preparing, 51-52
People, 8
Performance control, 12
Performance improvement, 12

Performance measurement, types of 1,
Performance planning, 12
Performance research and development, 10
Performance research and development department, role of, 12
Plan
    correcting, 33
    developing, 31-32
    implementing, 33
Problem analyses, 31
Problem-solving techniques, 27
    analysis of data, 31
    corrections to plan, 33
    developing plan, 31-32
    developing solutions, 31
    gathering data, 30
    identification of problem, 28-30
    implementing plan, 33
    problem scenario, 28
Process definition, 19
    material flow diagrams, 22-24
    organizational chart, 19-22
    simplified block diagrams, 24-26
Product definition, 13-15
    attributes, 15-16
    operating conditions, 17
    risks in, 18
    variables, 16-17
Product developers, 2, 3, 4, 5
Product development departments, role of, 2
Product specification, 16

Q
Quality
    application of, to business, 4-5
    definition of, 1-2, 9, 10
Quality audits, 10

Quality department, role of, 2, 10, 11
Quality specifications, 14, 17

R
Range, 38
    control limits for sample, 42-43
Resources, 6

S
Simplified block diagrams, 24-26
Solutions, developing, 31
Standard deviation, 38
Statistical methods, 35
    control charts, 39-61
    measures of location, 36-37
    measures of variation, 38-39
Strategy, 6
Success rate, 1
System, 10

T
Tasks, 8
Testing and packaging process standard symbol for, 24
Time line chart, 32
Transformation, 8
Transformation process, 6-8

U
u' chart, 50
    sample, 59
    steps in, 58
Unified quality theory, 2, 4, 10
Upper control limit, 42

V
Variable(s), 16-17
    definition of, 13
Variable control charts
    average and range chart, 43-44
    average and standard deviation

chart, 44-46
individuals and moving range
    chart, 48-50
median and range chart, 46-48
Variance, 38
Variation measures, 38
    range, 38
    standard deviation, 38
    variance, 38